The Pearl of God's Eye

Simone Oliver

The Pearl of God's Eye

A Fresh View of Biblical Women and God's Love for Us

Simone Oliver

The Pearl of God's Eye
Copyright © 2019 by Black Olive Press

Black Olive Press

All rights reserved.
ISBN 978-1-7338-3470-4

Printed in USA

Scripture taken from the CONTEMPORARY ENGLISH VERSION copyright© 1995 by the American Bible Society. Used by permission.

Scripture taken from The Expanded Bible. Copyright ©2011 by Thomas Nelson. Used by permission. All rights reserved.

Dedication

To SHARON AND Heidi who have been with me from the beginning and all the brave and bold women who have ventured with me through the ReVision Women Bible study as we re-imagined familiar stories and re-interpreted our lives. To Allen and Nicole, my loves, my muses and to God, my exceedingly great joy.

Praise for The Pearl of God's Eye

Simone Oliver is a "ReVisioned" woman and is helping other women re-vision themselves, too.

~ Jai Allen, Author of *In Realitea She is Me*

God is really using you to enlighten, encourage and empower women. I truly thank God for you and your ministry!!!

~ *Min. Heidi Cooper, Gary, IN*

Your voice is a necessary one to further inform and advance our current climate of Women Rising. Men and woman will be transformed by your ReVision [of Women in the Bible].

~ *Rev. Maureen Gerald, Interfaith Advisor & Moderator,*
United States Congress - New Jersey's 12th District

The world needs to hear what you have to say; broken, lost and hurting women are waiting to hear what you have to say! A message of love, hope, encouragement and healing. "The Pearl of God's Eye" is not church as usual, it's about getting to the very heart of what matters.

~ *Elizabeth Mitchell, Trenton, NJ*

Reverend Simone Oliver brings cogent clarity to voices we may have strained to hear otherwise. Please hear her!

~ Rev. Dr. Frank S. Morris,
Author of *Women Why Are You Weeping?*

Simone has used her insight to rally women to come out from the caves of despair, regret & silence; by grabbing hold of the validation that God has provided for us through Christ. Reverend Oliver draws from ancient examples to reinforce the need for women to stand up, speak out and Re-vision their lives!

~ Rev. Temaris Moore, Educator,
New York City Public Schools

Contents

Preface xi
Introduction 1
1: Achsah 5
2: Bathsheba 9
3: Deborah 17
4: Esther 23
5: Eve 31
6: Hagar 37
7: Hannah 43
8: Jael 49
9: Mary 55
10: The Samaritan Woman 61
11: Tamar 67
12: Vashti 73
13: Woman with the Issue of Blood 79
14: Women of Judges 19 85
15: Zelophehad's Daughters 93
Some Final Thoughts 99
About the Author 103
Works Cited 105

Preface

THIS PROJECT BEGAN as a simple discussion or, more accurately, a lament. A lament about being a woman in the church and feeling invisible, a bit inferior and being frustrated about it. It was about how we take on many responsibilities and find few seats at that table and even when we are at the table, our voices are often unheard. It was about how interpretations of our stories somehow left us feeling dispirited instead of encouraged and empowered.

Soon the conversation turned to leaving church altogether and then to creating spaces for women who love God but struggle with church. The task became to create a space that would re-imagine and re-interpret the lives of Biblical women and address some of the contemporary issues of women's lives.

From that pain and frustration, ReVision Women, an online Bible study for women, was birthed in January 2016. Since its inception, we have attracted women from Connecticut, the Carolinas, Indiana, Missouri, New Jersey, New York, Tennessee, Virginia, Iran and Pakistan.

Initially, I created each Bible study based on a specific woman and provided participants with outline, related articles and questions to ponder for self-reflection or discussion. I wanted to inspire and strengthen women in ways that they were not often inspired in their churches. I wanted to dispel myths and challenge stereotypes and assure them that there were many "places" for them in the world and in God's plan for humanity. But beyond anything, my greatest desire was to propel women into an intimate relationship with the God I knew loved them fiercely. I wanted them to know that God's grace is enough, and they are loved beyond comprehension.

It is now 2019 and we are still gathering in our sacred, cyber-space and though our studies have expanded, our goal remains to encourage, empower and inspire women through the word of God.

Introduction

A PEARL IS SYMBOLIC of wisdom gained by experience. It is a precious gem of great value. I believe the stories of women's lives are like pearls. They have tremendous value and can impart great wisdom to others. But, too often women's stories are covered with silence and shame. As a result, many women find no healing. I have often wondered, "Is there no Balm in Gilead for us?"

With that question in mind, I wrote this book for every woman who is on the verge of leaving church. Women who don't often hear stories of women preached or taught and when they do, they are usually not very positive or uplifting. Women who have been silenced, shamed and never invited into inquiry. Yet, I have found whenever given opportunity, they have so much to say. These are women whose sensibilities have been sharpened by their scars. Women who are reaching for God and searching for a relevant word that will transform their lives. These are women who long for God but can no longer tolerate the oppression of religion as usual.

The Pearl of God's Eye is the response to two simple questions: What can we learn from women in the Bible that can help us re-imagine our lives in ways that are inspiring? What can these ancient women teach us about the issues that afflict and affect us today? *The Pearl of God's Eye* shares the wisdom and experience of fifteen women in the Bible whose stories, I believe, bear witness to the lives of women everywhere, especially women of color. It bears witness to stories of women's lives who have remained loyal to the church but whose beings don't often reflect the abundant living that Jesus offered.

These are the women who are often found leading praise and worship on Sunday morning after being battered and abused on Saturday night. They often serve in the church kitchen while secretly aching for a "bun in their oven." They carry the misery and melancholy of miscarriages while caring for children in the nursery. They shout HALLEUJAH with HIV and more. They silently wonder if there no Physician in the house? Is there no Balm in Gilead?

I am persuaded that God has heard every woman's cry and desires that she be made whole. In Jesus Christ ALL things are made new. I pray that reading this book will bring healing and assurance that you, too, are valuable. In fact, you are the pearl of God's eye.

"Then the one sitting on the throne said: I am making everything new. Write down what I have said. My words are true and can be trusted." (*Contemporary English Version*, Rev. 21:5)

1
ACHSAH

THE COURAGE TO ASK
BACKGROUND TEXT: JOSHUA 15:13-19; JUDGES 1:11-15

THE STORY OF Achsah reminds me of a quote that has been attributed to Oprah Winfrey, "You get in life what you have the courage to ask for." Certainly, God affirms this truth in Matthew 7: 7-8 that says, "Ask, and the gift is yours. Seek, and you'll discover. Knock, and the door will be opened for you. For every persistent one will get what he asks for. Every persistent seeker will discover what he longs for. And everyone who knocks persistently will one day find an open door."

Achsah's brief story is a story that reminds us of the power of asking. Achsah is the daughter of the valiant and courageous Caleb. That is Caleb of Joshua and Caleb fame. The dynamic duo who, when sent to spy on the promised land, came back to Moses and said confidently, "We can take it." The other spies were far less confident and reported that they were like grasshoppers compared to the sons of Anak who inhabited the land of Debir.

Caleb issued a challenge to all the mighty warriors of Israel. Whoever could conquer the land of Debir would be given his daughter, Achsah, to marry. According to Jewish midrash, Achsah was beautiful. The meaning of her name suggested "whoever sees her is angry with his wife." Yes, indeed, she was good-looking and because of her beauty, men were willing to go to war with the Anakites to win her.

It turned out that Achsah's cousin, Othniel, took the land and Caleb gave his daughter to be his wife. After the marriage, Achsah urged her husband to allow her to ask her father for a field and he agreed. So, she approached her father on her donkey, got down and ask him to give her a gift. Since he had already given them Negeb, a very dry land, as a dowry, she asked that he also give her the springs of Upper and Lower Gulloth, and Caleb obliged.

Many commentators have argued that her asking was an act of greed and ingratitude. I would like to suggest instead that she was wise and practical. Negeb was a very dry land and if they were to live a favorable life and raise a family as expected, they needed irrigation. In her asking, she circumvented the patriarchal rule of law that passed land only to male heirs.

What we learn from her story is the power of "the ask." There can be many reasons that prevent us from asking for what we want or need. Often it is the fear of rejection, putting the needs of others ahead of our own, being hesitant and feeling powerless or believing that people should just know what we need that keeps us paralyzed and stagnant. We cannot expect people to possess the superhero skill of reading our minds.

We must remember that the reward is greater than the risk and if we do not ask God for what we want, the answer will always be no. Here are some things to keep in mind when asking. First, be clear on what you want, communicate it well and finally, know that you do not have to "deserve" it if you want it. Wanting it is enough.

Surely, God knows what we need but over and over, we are admonished to ask. James 4:2 says, "You want something you don't have, and you will do anything to get it. You will even kill! But you still cannot get what you want, and you won't get it by fighting and arguing. You should pray for it."[1] Words are powerful. They shape our existence. When we ask, we conspire with heaven to manifest our requests and bring them to pass.

2
Bathsheba

When Men Abuse Their Power
Background texts: Deuteronomy 22:22-27; Leviticus 20:10-21; 2 Samuel 11 & 12

I ONCE HEARD THAT the truest test of integrity is not what you do when no one is looking, but how you treat people when you have power. I like that definition because the temptation to abuse power is everywhere. We find government officials who are elected to work for the good of all people yet, those officials often exploit them. There are clergy persons who are too soon given unearned trust simply because of the position they hold who take undue advantage of the most vulnerable among their members. I have seen employers exert power over employees, teachers over students, police officers over civilians, men over women and parents over children. Americans seem to have a grisly lust for power.

Two of the most sacred and trusted positions

are the police officer and the clergy person. But we have repeatedly found that those trusts are blatantly shattered. Some things just should not be, such was the case of Police Officer Daniel Holtzclaw of Oklahoma City, Oklahoma. Holtzclaw is a serial rapist serving time for multiple counts of rape, sexual battery, forcible oral sodomy and other repulsive charges.

His victims were urban women of color whom he thought to have some petty criminal histories and would be afraid to report the crime for fear of outstanding warrants or other charges. (Un)Fortunately, he attempted to attack the wrong woman! He thought she fit his target type, but she did not. She was simply passing through the city and filed the police report that began the investigation that led to Holtzclaw's conviction. During his trial, a sixteen-year-old victim was asked why she did not report the crime. Her sobering and poignant response was, "What kind of police do you call on the police?"

Bathsheba was like so many of us who bear the weight of untold stories. She carried the burden of shame, blame, and humiliation simply because she was a woman in the world. Like so many women, her voice was snatched and silenced, covered up by a veil of romance simply because it led her to marriage.

When we take off our traditional religious lenses and end our romance with the text, we find Bathsheba's story is quite complex. All my life I was taught that she was a woman who lusted after the handsome King David and his goods. After all, isn't that what every girl wants? A man with power, position, and money? From Disney to Dynasty, this is supposed to be every girl's dream.

Let's begin by talking about David. David was a man favored by God and God promised to establish his throne and kingdom forever. Not only did David have the reputation of being a warrior who had victories over the Philistines, Moab, Hadadezer, and Edom, but he also annihilated 20,000 Syrians. Besides all that, David had about 300 wives and concubines. Despite his love for women, being a man after God's own heart caused the Lord to preserve David wherever he went, and he was trusted to keep the best interest of the people at heart as king and judge of all the people.

It was customary for kings to go to battle every spring, but during this spring, David elected to forgo the battle and remain at home in Jerusalem. At this point, he had few enemies, and he felt a bit confident and relaxed. Getting out of bed one evening, he walked onto the balcony and saw Bathsheba bathing.

Perhaps he caught a glimpse of Bathsheba by moonlight. That may sound romantic for some, but it wasn't a bath as we know it. It was neither relaxing nor sensual, but it was a ritual bath, a cleansing after menstruation. It's the last step in the purification process when a woman ceremonially dips into the Mikvah (bathtub built with rigid specs, four feet deep and filled with water from a natural source) while reciting a special prayer. Once this is completed, a Jewish woman is considered purified and spiritually refreshed. With 300 wives and concubines, this process was not new to David.

David asked around the castle to find out who she was. The response comes back that she is the daughter of Eliam and wife of Uriah. This was quite puzzling to me. Her husband was an officer in David's army and her grandfather, Ahithophel, was one of David's mighty warriors. David is aware that she is married but, the Bible says, "Then David sent messengers, and took her, and she came to him…"

Clearly, he sent more than one person to "take" her, which suggests that she was physically overpowered. So, she went to him because she had no choice. Besides that, he was the king and there was an imbalance of power that automatically removed her consent. Yes, he *took* her, and he *lay* with her, and she went home.

We can ask all the traditional questions: Why didn't she scream? Why didn't she resist? Why didn't she tell her husband? We can also raise other questions that might give us insight into how she behaved: Was she intimidated by his power and authority? How does one woman resist two or more men? Would her husband blame her? Would her husband lose his job? Whatever she imagined; I don't believe she could have possibly imagined what was to come.

Soon after, Bathsheba found that she was pregnant. There was no question about paternity because her husband had been at war, so she sent someone to tell David. He was a bit rattled and tried to cover his tracks by bringing Uriah home from battle to "wash his feet," which is a euphemism for laying with his wife. His scheme was foiled when Uriah did not return home but, slept at the door of the king's house. Uriah's loyalty to the king and his army outweighed his desire for his wife.

Then David contrived a more despicable plan. He plotted Uriah's murder. What made this act vile even among murderers was that he wrote a letter to Joab, the captain of the army and instructed him to leave Uriah to be killed and had Uriah deliver it. How low can you go, David? The letter instructed Joab to put Uriah on the front line in the heat of the battle, and then leave him without back up so that he could die. Joab did as he was directed. This was cold-blooded murder.

After a period of mourning, David brought Bathsheba to his castle, married her, and she eventually bore him two sons. Now here's where we are supposed to get elated and filled with joy. Bathsheba became the wife of the king, a rich, good-looking man of power and influence. After all, isn't that what every woman wants? Just think, she gets to live in **his** castle with all **his** stuff. Isn't that a wonderful life?

Well, maybe it isn't because "the thing David had done displeased the Lord." Yes, it seemed that life would go on as usual. That was until Nathan showed up and awakened David's God-consciousness by telling him a story about a rich man who had many flocks and herds but stole a poor man's "one little ewe lamb." David was so incensed by the story he ordered the culprit to restore to the man four times what was taken. God spoke through the prophet, tapped David on his outraged, arrogant shoulder and I imagine the prophet smiled, pointed his double-barreled index fingers at David, gave him a nod and said, "You are the man."

The Lord spoke to David like a disappointed father and said, that He had given much to David and he could have even had more if he just asked but, instead he despised God's commandment to do this evil. God meted out the consequences by letting David know that, because he had despised God and taken Uriah's wife to be his own wife, he and his family would have nothing but trouble. God would take David's wives right in front of his eyes and give them to his neighbor to lay with in broad daylight. Now, we don't usually hear about that part of the story. God took the assault and the murder personally. Even though David repented, and his life was spared, life as he knew it was never the same. He would never again have peace in his own home.

We are most often led to believe that Bathsheba came out a winner because she got the king and his castle, but we must consider all that she lost. First and foremost, she lost her first-born son. Despite David's repentant fasting and prayers, the first son died soon after birth. Also, I believe that the sexual assault caused her to lose her sense of being safe in the world and trusting others was no longer easy. She was left humiliated, powerless, isolated and afraid. She lost her husband and the home she shared with him. She lost her autonomy. She did not choose to be David's wife; she was chosen. She lost the dreams and plans she had for the future with her husband, Uriah. She lost friends and community when she moved from the old neighborhood into the castle. She went from being one man's wife to being one of many wives to a man. She had to endure being the wife of the man who raped her and murdered her husband and then bear his children. The insult to all her injuries was to bear the grief of losing *her* baby, although the text only refers to the baby as David's.

We talk about this story as if it were a consensual

relationship or some sordid affair that was instigated by Bathsheba. Often, she is made the sinner and we bolster the idea that David's behavior is acceptable, implying that all men can behave this way. We don't often hear of David's harsh punishment or the fact is God took the assault personally. I am reminded of the words of Jesus, "Whenever you did it for any of my people, no matter how unimportant they seemed, you did it for me." (Matthew 25:40)[2] God cares about us so much that every offense to us is an offense to God.

Despite Bathsheba's experience, through her marriage to David, the Lord established her in the bloodline of Jesus Christ. God blesses her to bear her second son, Solomon, to take the throne and become the wisest and wealthiest king in the world.

Bathsheba, like so many of us, bears the weight of untold stories that tell of shame, blame, and humiliation. Her body was not her own and her voice was cemented in silence. However, like Bathsheba, we have the assurance that we are seen and known by the God who will avenge us and work all things together for our good and God's glory.

3
DEBORAH

CALLED TO LEAD
BACKGROUND TEXT: JUDGES 4, 5

Deborah's story is just so exciting, especially for women like me who have been gifted to lead. Instead of being perceived as bossy, brassy and outspoken, Deborah lets us know that there are many ways to interpret power, and her willingness and ability to lead men in war took nothing from her being a wife and a nurturer.

Deborah was appointed the fourth judge of Israel after the death of Joshua. She found favor with God and among the people because while all of Israel had forsaken the way of the Torah, she was steadfast and resolute in her commitment to God. She was not only a judge but a prophet and a wife. She was a well-rounded woman who brought a great deal of wisdom and insight to her work.

She was the example of a healthy relationship with God; she lets us know that God uses women in *big* ways. She was the vessel that God used to speak instruction and inspiration to Barak. Although he was the captain of the army, he seemed to be a bit reticent about moving the army forward on his own. He refused to go to war without her.

It's hard to guess whether Barak was afraid to go on his own or if her influence as the local judge and prophet simply earned her the highest respect. Either way, he wanted her guidance. So, she agreed to go to war with him but assured him that this was going to be a girl's game! He would get no credit for the victory. The battle was going to be won at the hands of another woman, Jael, who was not even an Israelite.

Barak summons his leaders and 10,000 men to battle, and Deborah goes with them. Sisera, the captain of the opposing army, gets word of their coming and prepares his men for battle. Deborah instructs Barak to go forward because the Lord has gone before him. Sisera flees on foot, and Barak demolishes his army. Through this exchange, we can see why Deborah is celebrated as the "Mother of Israel" for she is unyielding and inspires courage.

The Song of Deborah (Judges 5:1-9) memorializes her as the "Mother of Israel." Not only is she an unyielding force, but she also exhibits the qualities of loving patience, influence, sacrifice, perseverance and faith throughout the narrative. Although her leadership was enveloped in motherhood, we can't be sure that she had any child of her own.

Some suggest that this tribute as a Mother of Israel was done to minimize her leadership and keep her "in her place" as a subordinate to men. That idea might contain some truth but perhaps conversely, we can choose to allow it to exalt motherhood as a high level of leadership equal to or surpassing military leadership, and indeed, I believe it is! After all, motherhood is prone to protect life; the military is prone to extinguish it.

We don't often hear sermons or sit in Bible studies that highlight the leadership gifts of Deborah or her ministry as prophet and judge to the people of Israel. It is interesting that God chooses her to judge at a time when Israel has turned away from God and is being ruled by the Canaanites. Perhaps she is chosen because of her moral compass and like a mother, her ability to influence the people under her care. She exudes the nurturing qualities of an encourager, intercessor, and champion of the people.

In the Song of Deborah, she sings of Israel being desolate until she rose up as "a mother of Israel." So much for modesty! For her, leadership and motherhood are synonymous as they rightly should be. She leads by godly instruction and example, sheltering the nation from danger as she goes to war with Barak. She cares enough to be firm and resolute, telling him that he will get no glory in this battle. I believe she says that to encourage him to fight because it's the right thing to do and not for self-glory.

This story upsets the apple cart of gender roles that the society laid before women from birth when boys and girls are separated by pink and blue blankets. The idea of a woman being gentle, subservient and demure is replaced by a woman who is decisive, proactive, candid, exacting and powerful.

What I love most about the story is that it does not force us to choose. We don't have to choose between motherhood and leading beyond the home. We don't have to choose between preaching the gospel or being a wife. It's not a matter of choosing to be strong or weak, powerful or delicate. It is never either/or but it is both and as Deborah's power and influence are juxtaposed with the nurturing qualities of motherhood.

Deborah's story permits us to find our places wherever we fit–from the battlefield to the boardroom but finding our places in the world is not without consequence. In 1973, the volunteer military opened opportunities for women to be of service and just three years later, US military academies began to admit women. It was sometime later when women began to be sent into the combat zone, serving on ships and flying combat missions. They also began to rise into important leadership positions during the time of the Iraq and Afghanistan wars. They are continuing to rise to senior leadership in all the services.

The 1970's not only opened up opportunities for women in the military, but changes in social trends supporting legislation also opened avenues of movement for women in the private sector. Women began to make their way up the corporate management ranks and were finding their way into the boardroom.

Women are still not making significant strides on the executive level. Some reasons are that the world does not value the differences between men and women. What women bring to the table still does not hold the weight and merit of men. Women have a stronger pull towards family and life commitments that clash with the demands of the workplace. Let us face it, women are still marginalized, sidelined and suppressed.

Even with opportunities and advancement for women in the military and the world of work, working is not without consequences for women because claims of unfair treatment and sexual harassment abound. Perhaps this has been the incentive for women to move into entrepreneurship. Forbes magazine has noted entrepreneurship as the new women's movement.[3] Women are finding ways to balance family and work by creating business that allow them to set their own schedules and determine their own priorities.

Have you ever been caught between the push and pull of motherhood and ministry, motherhood and the military or motherhood and management? Me too. Giving too much attention to work makes you feel you're letting your family down, and too much attention to family makes you feel like you're slacking in business.

Deborah reminds us that we don't have to choose. Maybe we should not be reluctant to ask for more support where needed, but we don't have to choose. We can have it your way.

4
ESTHER

HOLY AUDACITY: INTERCESSION, INTERVENTION AND DELIVERANCE
BACKGROUND TEXT: ESTHER 2:12-23; 4:1-17

THE POWER OF Esther's story rests in the fact that a once voiceless and powerless woman finds autonomy not only to assert her independence, but to save a nation. Her life is the demonstration of what it means to sacrifice one's own comfort to advocate for the good of others. Esther used her platform to demand justice for her people and pleaded the cause of the Jews before God in heaven and the King on earth.

Esther was a Hebrew in exile who grew up in the home of her cousin, Mordecai. She lives in a Jewish community in Persia where King Ahasuerus ruled. When Vashti, his queen, was banned from the kingdom for refusing to display her beauty before a drunken king and his cohorts, Esther, who is said to be quite stunning, was one of many beautiful virgins taken from neighboring provinces and groomed as a possible replacement of Queen Vashti.

God is never mentioned in the story, but we can see God's movement through a series of ironic events. Esther goes from an orphan to a queen; the Jews who are targeted for genocide become victorious over their enemies; and the pit dug for Mordecai becomes the very pit that devours his adversary.

It is the planned annihilation of the Jews that fuels Esther's faith and gives her the holy audacity to call for a fast among all Jews to pray that she seeks and finds the favor of the king. God's providence is seen when God delivers Esther and the Jews from a government-sanctioned genocide. God reveals his unfailing love and grace for God's people and the ability to reverse the deeds meant to destroy us and to work them for our good.

Esther's story is often told as the story of a very lucky or blessed woman (depending on whose doing the telling) who wins the king's heart and embarks on a wonderful life of luxury as his queen. Of course, that is where we are supposed to celebrate again–every woman wants a powerful man and his goods. Then for a greater wow-factor, she's used by God, saves a nation and goes down in history. Pretty good for a mere woman, right? Still, let's consider all the issues around her story.

An announcement went out to 127 provinces looking for a replacement for Queen Vashti, who was booted out of the kingdom for dishonoring the king. Basically, the king's men feared that women all over the kingdom would become defiant if there were no consequences for Vashti's refusal to appear before the king. The king mandated that beautiful virgins from the 127 provinces be gathered and brought to Shushan, the capital city, kept in the custody of the king's eunuchs and given beauty treatments for a year to prepare for a night with the king. The one who pleased him most would be the one he made the queen. Esther gained his favor and was made the queen.

Let's examine this story a bit more closely and catch sight of what's being overlooked in the telling. While we may be favored by God, we are still often marginalized and mistreated in the world. Esther did not have a choice. No. She was taken! In fact, 127 women were taken. In today's world, we call that human trafficking.

Depending on your view, you can say that these women were very fortunate to have the opportunity to compete, yes compete, for the position of Queen. Even if they somehow didn't measure up, most likely they would remain in the king's harem as his concubines and be taken care of. However, you could also conclude that they lost the one quality that makes us human. The freedom to choose.

It's most likely that they lost their virginity to the king as the text indicates each woman went to the king's palace in the evening and returned to the women in the morning. Let me suggest that they had a little more than dinner. Each woman spent the night with the king and lost her virginity without her consent to someone she did not know, did not care about and who did not care for her. Each woman would be returned to the king's harem and from that time forward, she could never choose a lover, where she would live or how she would manage each day. It was quite possible to remain in the harem and never be called into the king's quarters again. So, as we focus on Esther, let's remember the other women/sisters who started the journey with her. Let's also remember that some things written in the scripture are the reflection of the society and not the heart of God.

Unlike her sister-friends, Esther found favor from the beginning. She was destined for great things when Hegai, the women's custodian, found favor in her immediately. He gave her extra beauty preparations, seven choice servants and moved her into the best room in the house. When it was her time to spend the night with the king, she took only the things that Hegai advised, and she delighted everyone who saw her. As the story goes, the king loved her and gave her the crown that was once Vashti's. Esther took the advice of her uncle Mordecai and never revealed her Jewish nationality to the king. Some scholars believe Esther may have been endangered had she not hidden her identity from the king.

Haman was appointed chief prince among the princes of Persia. King Xerxes commanded all the subjects in the kingdom to bow to Haman as they would the king. Esther's uncle, Mordecai refused to bow, and Haman hated him. Haman's ego was so badly bruised by one man, he put forth an edict, with the King's approval, that every Jew in the Persian kingdom be killed. Mordecai called on Esther to act on behalf of all the Jews.

Initially, Esther felt powerless and afraid because no one was allowed into the king's presence without being summoned. Unless the king was gracious and extended his scepter, she would be killed. She instructed Mordecai to call on all the Jews to a fast on her behalf and through fasting and prayer she was empowered to see the king. The favor of God rested on her life yet again, and she walked in to see the king with confidence, power, authority, and wisdom for she knew she had been called for "such a time as this." The king graciously extended his sceptor and welcomed her presence. As he extended his scepter,

Esther extended her heart and hands. She alone held the hope of salvation and deliverance for the Jewish people. Her appointment with the king was filled with favor. Instead of a government sanctioned genocide, she saved her life, Mordecai's life and the lives of her people. Ultimately, Haman was hanged from the same gallows that was planned for Mordecai's hanging.

Like Esther, women are mobilizing globally to save nations. The US Women's March in 2017 was the backlash against the patriarchy and the utter disrespect and disdain for women exhibited by the Trump administration. Over five million people participated in the march to send a no-nonsense message to the President and legislators. The March advocated for human rights, women's rights, health care reform and a myriad of other concerns. There were 408 marches in US cities and 167 marches around the world.

The group is currently led by a diverse cadre of women, Tamika D. Mallory, Bobby Bland, Carmen Perez, Linda Sarsour and Janaye Ingram, who send clear messages that women do matter, and the strength of our voices will bring change. Indeed, "We are the leaders we have been waiting for."

Do you feel that you have been left without a voice? Connect with a women's group that has similar interests as yours and find the support of like-minded companions and friends. Whether you choose to run for office or support those who do, we can win.

5
Eve

The Pursuit of Knowledge
Background text: Genesis 1-3

Since 1982, the number of women obtaining bachelor's degrees in the US has outnumbered men, and since 2005, women have attained the greatest number of advanced degrees as well. Sadly, our sisters in developing and poor countries have not been as fortunate.

While more girls and women globally are getting an education than ever before, many are still denied the opportunity of being educated. Without an education, many girls have limited opportunities, are forced into lives of poverty and are at risk for sex trafficking and other forms of exploitation. When we fail to educate girls, we limit the economic opportunities of families and nations.

In our discussion of Eve, sin *is not* the issue that

we will focus on. How can we possibly deny her sin? Even if we wanted to, the world wouldn't let us, and neither would the church! For this discussion, we'll be looking at her person and what might have motivated her choices.

Women around the world still bear the brunt of Eve's sin and punishment. Her story has been interpreted (primarily by men) in ways that still diminish women. It seems to be presented that Adam was restored through the finished works of Christ, but Eve somehow remained guilty and consequently inferior.

With that in mind, women are most often taught that Eve represents everything a good man should guard against. This one woman's sin now represents deception, disobedience, selfishness, being weak-willed and disloyal among other things. Of course, we all know men who exhibit these same negative characteristics.

Some scholars suggest there are two accounts of the creation story in our Bible. The first, in Genesis Chapter 1, focuses on the broad framework of events. In it, God creates the vegetation, then the animals and finally man and woman as one. The second account, found in Genesis Chapter 2, focuses on humanity. In it, God creates humans, the plants and then the animals and later separates the humans into male and female. It is in Chapter 2 that the Lord gave the command to Adam to eat freely of every tree in the garden but not of the tree of the knowledge of good and evil. If Adam did eat, then the consequence would be death. It is in Chapter 2 that God made Adam a comparable (*equal, a match for, as good as*) partner. This made Adam responsible for passing on the important information that would give life or bring death.

When the serpent slithered up to Eve to engage her in a bit of conversation, she absolutely knew which trees she could and could not eat from and told him so! She even took it upon herself to embellish a bit by adding, "We can't even touch it, or we'll die."

Yet the thought of really knowing, of being like God, knowing everything from good to evil was alluring. Eve seemed to have an insatiable curiosity and got a little stirred and animated when she realized that just by eating the fruit of one tree, she could know everything. Yes, indeed it could make her wise.

Eve offered the fruit to Adam and they both ate. Wait, wait, wait! Didn't Adam get the commandment? He does not remind her about the instructions or chastise her about eating from the tree, but instead he takes the fruit and freely eats it.

Soon, God comes around as God usually did–in the evening, in the cool of the day. God confronted them by asking why they were naked and what had happened? Adam blamed Eve and indirectly blamed God for giving Eve to him. By contrast, Eve was candid and forthright—she confessed her sin that she was beguiled by the serpent.

God cursed the serpent and punished Adam and Eve with pain and labor. The punishment for Eve was pain in childbirth and subordination to Adam. This lets us know that God's original intent was equality of the sexes. So, if faith in the finished work of Christ restored us to our original relationship to God, then it would be reasonable to assume it also restored the status of women to God's original intent.

The thought of learning and knowing still drives girls and women all over the world. One such girl was Malala Yousafzai who defied the Taliban, demanding that all girls in Pakistan be allowed to receive an education. As she stood up for education, she was shot by a Taliban gunman for her efforts. After surviving her attack, Malala had this to say, "The terrorists thought that they would change our aims and stop our ambitions, but nothing changed in my life except this: weakness, fear, and hopelessness died. Strength, power and courage were born." Malala became the youngest Nobel Peace Prize winner at age seventeen.

In the United States, African American women face a unique and unfortunate reality. They have quickly become the most educated demographic in the country; however, in health, wellness, housing, economic stability and violence, they have the lowest statistical outcomes.

While remaining the most loyal supporters of the church, one in five Black women have been raped. They suffer violence at the hand of intimate partners at a rate of three times that of white women and comprise 64% of new HIV diagnoses nationally. They are more likely to die in childbirth than Hispanic and White women and suffer disproportionately from diabetes, high blood pressure and heart disease.[4] In many ways, education has not empowered African American women. These important issues are rarely addressed in religious spaces.

Like Eve, we are born with inquiring minds. We were made just that way from the beginning. Girls and women around the world are hungering for knowledge. It costs societies across the globe much more to *not educate* girls than to provide them with quality educations. Empowering girls by educating them improves their health and quality of life as well as the lives of their families and their communities. It also positively impacts the economic development of a nation. The Contemporary English Version (CEV) of Proverbs 18:15, says, "Everyone with good sense wants to learn." Indeed. I believe if we educate women and girls, we can change the world.

6
Hagar

Never Alone
Background text: Genesis 16; Genesis 17:20-21, Genesis 21:9-17; Genesis 25:12

Hagar is a young, single, immigrant, domestic worker who becomes a mother. Her status as a slave left her vulnerable to the whims of Sarah, her mistress and Abraham, Sarah's husband. Hagar, just like so many undocumented domestic workers, found herself at the mercy and fancy of those who employed her.

The Lord had promised Sarah and Abraham a son in their old age, a son from whom God would make a great nation. Sarah, feeling the scorn and humiliation of being childless, became impatient when it did not happen as she expected. Though God's time is not our time, she decided to give her slave-girl, Hagar, to Abraham and have her son through her servant.

It wasn't an unusual practice. In fact, it was common and customary in the culture for a woman who was infertile to gain an heir through her servant. What was problematic was that she refused to wait for the promise of God and took the matter into her own hands. Abraham didn't argue about it. He did as Sarah requested, and Hagar bore him a son who was named Ishmael.

Whenever we operate outside of the will of God, things get complicated. So it was, things didn't turn out quite as Sarah expected. In fact, after Hagar conceived the child, she despised Sarah. The Bible says, "she looked with contempt on her mistress."

Typically this is interpreted to mean that Hagar somehow felt superior to Sarah because she was pregnant, and Sarai could not get pregnant. It seems that men and children are always the prizes that women are supposed to jockey for. Men and children are always the measure by which women are to establish their worth.

But could it be that Hagar felt used and resentful? Could it be that she trusted Sarah to protect her (she was a young girl) and she felt betrayed? Maybe she was weary of being a commodity traded-off at the hands of those more powerful than she? It's certainly something to think about. Perhaps every woman doesn't see scoring men/husbands and having children as the end game of life.

At any rate, Sarah is provoked and angry, although she appears to take no responsibility for what she chose to initiate. She was clearly appalled by Hagar's behavior and attitude toward her and cursed Abraham. "Let the wrong done to me be on you." Huh? Okay, Sarah, get a hold of yourself! You took the plunge down this slippery slope!

Abraham accepted no culpability in the matter and left Sarah to deal with Hagar as she chose. Sarah was so harsh that Hagar decided to just run away without money or food. An uncertain future appeared to be more enticing than a life threatened by Sarah's anger and bitterness.

Hagar ran a great distance–right into the wilderness and right into the arms of God. She found herself by a spring and it is there that she saw God. God called her by name and asked her where she was coming from and where she was going. Hagar could only say from where and why she was running. She had no idea where she was going.

Have you ever been there? Not sure just where you're going? I love the imagery of Hagar's encounter with God. It suggests that God can locate us in the worst situations and refresh us, but I don't think she was ready for God's instructions and so often, neither are we. "Go back to your mistress and be submissive." What God? Why? Hagar did what any sensible woman with no food, no money and a little of hope would do–she listened to God and went back to Sarah's household.

After fourteen years, Sarah gave birth to Isaac, the son of promise. Sarah saw Isaac and Ishmael playing together and demanded that Abraham put Hagar and Ishmael out. Abraham was a bit distressed, but God told him to do as Sarah said because true to his word, God was going to fulfill the promise and make a nation out of Abraham. Isn't it good to know that God is faithful even when we mess up?

Abraham woke up the following morning and packed a bag for Hagar and Ishmael of water and a small loaf of bread and sent them on their way. When she's out of water and out of bread, Hagar allows Ishmael to sleep. She moved on ahead of him because she could not face watching him die. But God heard the cries of Ishmael and opened Hagar's eyes to see a well of water. She filled her bottle, and they drank. Their lack did not destroy their lives because God was with them.

Although Hagar could not imagine, God had plans for Ishmael's life. God promised Hagar before she returned to Sarah's charge that Ishmael would be a "wild man." Ishmael would have a life of conflict, but he would live among his brethren. God also promised Abraham that Ishmael would be blessed and made fruitful. God promised to multiply Ishmael greatly and he would be a father to twelve princes and make a great nation.

We live in a society where single mothers are often demonized and accused of creating their own problems. Hagar's story challenges that notion. She, like so many, was a victim of circumstances not of her own choosing. Single moms tend to work more hours, lack support systems and too often must rely on precarious childcare options. They tend to earn lower wages and have compromised health care coverage and not all of this is their doing. Often their singleness is a result of divorce, separation or death of a spouse.

There is a constant pressure on singles moms to balance work with the time and energy it takes to parent their children. With a single income and the high cost of childcare, living in poverty is a common reality. The poverty rate for single mothers is about twice that of the national average.

Hagar's story is not only a story of seeing and being seen by God, but it compels us to consider just who is in God's purview. Hagar wasn't of the chosen. She wasn't an Israelite. Hagar didn't have a perfect life or the support of a loving family. Yet, God saw her, knew what she needed and was pleased to provide. God is still Jehovah Jireh, the God who provides.

I don't know about you, but that makes me want to shout with joy. God sees each of us and not one of us is out of God's reach. It is so easy to feel isolated and alone in our day-to-day struggles. The challenges of single parenting can seem endless. I hope you can find comfort in knowing that God is closer than we often realize. God know exactly what we need.

7
Hannah

The Struggle of Infertility
Background text: 1 Samuel 1

An infertility advocate described a woman's struggle to get pregnant as a "pain that is difficult to describe." Another woman succinctly summed up the matter as "soul crushing." Women who can't conceive often feel as though they are failures at the very thing that should come naturally and easily for women–pregnancy. They are often left feeling isolated, lonely and broken.

Treatment for infertility is a luxury that many cannot afford, but even for those who can, deciding to begin the process can be stressful. You see, once you decide to undergo infertility treatments, science erases your privacy and the intimacy of lovemaking. You share this experience with doctors, nurses, office staff, the pharmaceutical industry and hospital technicians. That is daunting!

Twelve percent of all women and one in eight couples are affected by infertility, but you can bet that nobody's talking about it in the women's ministry. Infertility is shrouded in feelings of being abnormal, feeling less than a woman, and it's covered up with shameful silence. The stigma of not disclosing family business forces many women to carry the burden alone without the support of family and friends.

I don't think anyone knows the deep and insatiable longing for a child except the one who knows that longing for herself, but I think we may all know what it is like to long for something to the point of pinning and sorrow. Hannah knew. Hannah's story has a happy ending. She gets her heart's desire. Many of our stories don't end that way, but God sends a strong message of God's sovereignty and faithfulness despite our circumstances. The process of time will always bring the needed change–sometimes the circumstances change and sometimes we are changed in the circumstances.

Hannah, a woman devoted to God, struggled with infertility in a world where her status and worth as a woman were based on being a wife and mother. She found herself painfully distressed especially because she was teased, mocked, tested and minimized by her husband Elkanah's second wife, Penninah.

Of course, Penninah was a baby factory! She was generously blessed with the ease of conception and plenty of children, but what Hannah does have that totally eludes Penninah is Elkanah's unwavering love. It was not enough. Hannah was so distressed that she made her way to the temple and became so engrossed in prayer that she behaved like she was drunk.

When Eli, the priest, chided her for her supposed drunkenness, she responded that her spirit was so broken that she was just pouring her heart out before the Lord. Have you ever been that broken? Eli blessed her and prayed that God would grant her heart's desire. From his lips to God's ears. God was moved by her cries and Eli's intercession and she became pregnant.

Not only was she pregnant, but she was pregnant with a son, an heir. She dedicated the baby, Samuel, to the Lord. Her story represents the struggle and derision of an infertile woman. It's no wonder why so many of us suffer in silence when we carry such a burden. But Hannah's story also represents great faith, the power of asking, and the power of intercession.

Childlessness is a difficult and disturbing fate for many women who carry the weight of social rejection and ridicule. These feelings of inadequacy are personified in Penninah, who taunted and mocked Hannah because there was no suckling at her breast. Hannah's home was silent, empty and childless.

Verse five of the text lets us know that it was God who had shut her womb. It reminds us that God is sovereign over all our affairs. Why God would choose to afflict her I do not know. Who among us knows the mind of God? Hannah certainly couldn't understand it. She bore a pain that even her faith and the unconditional love of her husband could not soothe. Not to mention, Penninah, her "rival," provoked her endlessly.

The language of "rival" is quite interesting. We live in a society that teaches women to compete–not in sports or other healthy ways, but to compete as if men and children are prizes to be vied for. What was it that Hannah really craved? Was it just a child, or could she also be longing for social status and acceptance? Living in these times, her worth was attached not only to her having a husband and his status, but also to her womb.

Hannah's longing for a child was so great that she would fall into depression, weeping and refusing to eat; she had become bitter. But her weeping and torment caused her to pour out her anguish to the Lord, the same God who sets the captives free and brings recompense to those who have suffered unjustly, and she made a deal.

She promised God that if God would look on her with kindness and give her a male child (male children brought status), that she would give him back to the Lord, offering the child as a Nazarite. It was this crying out in desperation, brokenness and misery that caused

Eli to believe she was drunk. I imagine that her prayer was so gut-wrenching that it moved Eli to give her a blessing and God to respond favorably to her cries.

Her story does not suggest that every prayer will be answered according to our desires, but it does affirm the sovereignty of God. It reminds us that God hears our prayers. She went to God with dashed hope and a desperate heart, but the blessings of Eli spoke restoration to her soul and God remembered Hannah.

We don't know what her process was or how much time it took, but she did conceive a child. This also reminds us that everything is a process. Everything has a season and we must learn to endure each changing season with as much joy as we can. Yet, the joy is not in the process itself, but the joy is in a faithful God.

God is faithful. God commanded man and woman to be fruitful and multiply (Genesis 1:28) and take dominion over the earth. With such a vast and profound charge issued to humanity, to be fruitful and multiply goes beyond childbearing. With that in mind, the benchmarks of womanhood go way beyond marriage and motherhood.

When we sow our gifts, talents and time into others and the causes we are passionate about, we are naturally fruitful and will multiply because we can be sure that whatever we sow will bring forth a harvest.

The harvest will be evident in the lives of others. We are reminded of this truth in Isaiah 54:1,4a.

> [1]Sing and shout,
> even though you have never
> had children!
> The LORD HAS PROMISED THAT YOU
> will have more children
> than someone married
> [4]Don't be afraid or ashamed
> and don't be discouraged.
> You won't be disappointed.

Our unfulfilled longings may be to have a child or may be to have a dream long deferred come to fruition. We must know that we are more than our husbands, offspring, and bodies. We are made in the image of God and are complete all by ourselves. Is there an unfulfilled longing that has driven you away from God? Remember, whether God deems it right to answer our prayers as we desire or not, our joy can be found in a God who is faithful, a God who does not forsake us but walks with us through it all.

8
JAEL

WOMAN WARRIOR
BACKGROUND TEXT: JUDGES 4, 5

Can you imagine what would happen if our daughters heard stories of strong girls and women who were not confined to gender roles, especially in Sunday church school? I absolutely love the stories of Jael and Deborah just for that reason. It is so wonderful to know that God approves of women warriors. Their stories empower us to know that God also loves and approves strong, assertive, and quick-witted women.

Jael was the wife of Herber, the Kenite, and a woman warrior who won the Lord's victory in what appeared to be a cruel and unusual way. Jael's character seemed to possess qualities that can be contrasted to Barak, whom Deborah lead into battle. Unlike Barak, who was reluctant to go to battle, Jael devised the strategy and initiated the violence that killed Sisera, the commander of the Canaanite army. That was the clever and skillful maneuver that gave the Israelites the victory.

Worn out from battle, Sisera sought a safe place to rest and Jael welcomed him into her tent. Parched and weary, all he wanted was a refreshing cup of water, but Jael gave him milk instead. Of course, warm milk (there's was no refrigeration) is a known sedative for the sleep deprived.

While he was sleeping, exhausted from what seemed to be a never-ending battle, she drove a spike through his temple. This killed him and fulfilled the prophecy that the Lord would give the victory into the hands of a woman.

Jael and Deborah are interesting because they displayed a blend of characteristics that are considered both masculine and feminine. They are both married, nurturing, strong, decisive and proactive. Jael is touted as a hero for attributes that are commonly despised in women. She was violent, aggressive, crafty and artful and she was celebrated for just that!

In the song of Deborah, Jael was celebrated as "blessed among women." Does this sound like anyone else you know? Yes. Mary, the mother of Jesus. Not only do they celebrate her as blessed, but they sing in detail of the cunning act of brutality and deliverance she committed.

The Pearl of God's Eye

The song of celebration also gives an account of the anxiety of Sisera's mother as she waited for his return from the battle. As she cried through her window wondering when he would be coming home, the wise women answered her and suggested that he may be finding and dividing the spoils, "to every man a girl or two." Women and children have been and yet remain the victims of war.

The attitudes of the wise women allude to rape as a weapon of war and suggest that women can be indoctrinated into a mind-set that makes us complicit in our oppression. They stand in sharp contrast to the clear and forthright actions of Jael.

As we consider military life today, women seem to carry a greater psychological burden than men. According to Washington Monthly[5], female soldiers are regularly harassed, assaulted and raped by fellow soldiers and commanding officers. They are also deployed while their infants and children remain at home. Upon their return, women veterans are at greater risk for homelessness, divorce, single parenting, and they may be more susceptible to psychological disorders, including PTSD, making it more difficult to reintegrate into the roles and responsibilities of being a mom, wife, girlfriend, daughter, and employee.

For many, this begs the question of whether women are fit to engage in war. Apparently, God believes they are. However, what really must be considered is the psychological burden that different gender expectations bring. Perhaps that is what makes women more susceptible to the trauma.

Despite its challenges, there are women that God calls and equips for military service. Jael's and Deborah's stories tell us so. If you are called to serve God and country in this way, you can be certain that God approves of your service. God is with you, fighting right beside you.

The Pearl of God's Eye

¹I praise you, LORD!
You are my mighty rock,
and you teach me
how to fight my battles.
²You are my friend,
and you are my fortress
where I am safe.

(Psalms 144:1-2)

9
Mary

A Mother's Joy, A Mother's Pain
Background text: Isaiah 61, Matthew 1:18-25; Luke 1:26-80, 2:1-52; John 19:25-27; Psalm 22

Mary's story is too often told with the romantic idealism that seems to remove her from the human sensibilities of motherhood. But it is necessary that we give voice to a woman who can be magnified in her humanity as well as her glory.

When we allow ourselves to visit her humanity, she tells a story of joy and sorrow. Mary tells a story of a divine and holy God who steps into the lives of ordinary people and does extraordinary things through them. That is her joy. She also tells of the excruciating pain of losing her first son to a violent empire that perceived him as an enemy of the state.

Mary was just an ordinary girl of about fourteen or

fifteen at the time of her engagement to Joseph and the conception of the Christ child. Her only distinction was that God found favor in her. Certainly, it was not a bad distinction. In our modern Christian culture, we have an overly fanciful notion of what it means to be favored by God. In fact, it can be a blessed gift that many times comes with great challenges.

Sometimes it seems God's favor is more troublesome than it is exhilerating. Mary was young, single and pregnant before marriage. She lived her early years as a poor immigrant and later witnessed her son's execution as an enemy of the state. Maybe when we look at Mary's story from the lens of her reality, we can find hope in a risen Savior and hope that without honor or distinction and in the face of difficult circumstances, we are loved and cared for by God.

Sometimes to be favored by God is to be disparaged and criticized by others. Mary was a young virgin, impregnated by an invisible God (Holy Spirit) just as she was about to get married. Well, favor sounds a bit fishy to me! We tell Mary's story as romantically as we tell most Bible stories about women, but the truth is that before Mary makes peace with her destiny, she is troubled and confused. I don't know how long it was before she finally submitted herself to God's will, but I would guess that it didn't happen when she was told she'd conceive a child by the Holy Spirit. Who could grasp that? Mary certainly couldn't! She wanted to know, "How could such a thing be possible?" She had never been with a man! I'm sure the fact that she was already committed to marrying a man she had not been intimate with concerned her and like any young, pregnant unwed girl, she worried about what she would tell her parents. Yet, the angel of the Lord said, "Rejoice, highly-favored one, the Lord is with you; blessed are you among women."

What? That sounds like trouble to me. Nevertheless, Mary submits to God and is blessed by the promise. Mary was young, single and poor but became the dwelling of the divine. God has a habit of showing up in ordinary places.

Mary soon found fellowship and consolation with her older cousin, Elizabeth, who was also pregnant against all odds. This is something we don't take time to consider, but this is a powerful moment. Elizabeth affirmed and supported Mary while they shared in the experience of supernatural pregnancy. This suggests that women should take time to connect with other women and especially older women when we are experiencing what seems to be impossible circumstances. Sometimes we need to connect with women who can affirm us and speak positively into our lives when we can't make much sense of our own messy circumstances.

Soon, Mary began to worship and testify of the Lord's favor upon her life. She prophesied about God's intervention in the doings of humanity and God's power to overturn the powers-that-be. She told of a God who is on the side of the poor and the powerless. She sang about a king and His kingdom that would turn the world upside down. She spoke of a time when the very system that oppresses the downtrodden would be overturned. That is Mary's joy.

In contrast, Mary was also burdened because she had to reconcile living the "now" and the "will be." She struggled with loving her first-born baby boy and his revealed destiny, for when Simeon laid eyes on the baby boy, he declared that his eyes had seen the Lord's salvation. Mary and Joseph were amazed by these things, but Mary was also burdened by the weight of the responsibility she carried.

When Jesus was twelve, Mary found him in the temple teaching, engaging the teachers of the law and leaving them astounded. He was beginning to come into his own. Can you imagine giving birth to a child, bringing your baby home to love and nurture knowing that he would soon die as a common criminal? An enemy of the state?

Just as the mothers of boys and men of color dread their children's interaction with law enforcement, Mary feared the jealousy of Herod the King. Like most

African American mothers and sons, I wonder if Mary and Jesus had "the talk." That talk that reminds African American boys that their black skin is an offence to others with the power to kill. For Mary and Jesus that talk would have focused on the fear and resentment of Jesus by government and religious powers because it was prophesied that he would be king.

Jesus' life was threatened from birth. He was a threat to the powers that be. Was it favor to know your child would die? We sanitize her story so much that we never feel her pain, but God knew her pain, just as God knows ours.

Mary loved her son so much that despite her suffering, she remained present to the needs of Jesus and stayed close to him even as he faced death on the cross. I imagine that her presence brought him some comfort in his distress as did John and the other women who stood by the cross with courageous resolve. Amid the disorder, Jesus gave her into the care of John, his disciple. Like any good son, he wanted to ensure the care for his mother's day-to-day existence. The symbolism, however, suggests she is not just his mother but the mother of the movement that he entrusted to the disciples. Mary is not only the mother of Jesus; she is also the Mother of the Church.

As she remained at the cross, this mother–mother of a son and mother of the Savior — was resolute in her commitment. She and the other women were not only consumed with the grief of such a heinous loss, but they were also in danger. There was social and political chaos and the military at every turn. There was tension everywhere. Who could be trusted? Yet, rising before dawn, Mary and the other women found their way to the tomb to anoint Jesus' body, but he is not there. They encounter an angel who announced, "He is risen, just as He said."

From Jesus' Father's heart, it was a mission. From his mother's heart it was a murder. Her heart could never grasp what her mind and spirit knew to be true. For His Father, it was finished. Salvation was accomplished for the world. For his mother, it was final. While she gained a Savior, she lost a son.

There are so many things we learn from Mary's story. First, God can meet us in ordinary conditions. We learn that blessings and favor bring unique challenges that are not always pleasant, but like Mary, we have the assurance that we will prevail. Just as the angel showed up at the tomb, God will meet us in seemingly dead situations. God will show up for you, no matter the circumstances.

10
The Samaritan Woman

A God Who Breaks Through
Background text: John 4:4-42

I believe this is one of the most powerful stories in the Bible. Sadly, it has been interpreted to be one of the most damning and damaging stories in the Bible for women. Far too often, the Samaritan Woman's story is imagined strictly from a contemporary male perspective.

Viewing the Samaritan Woman's story in the proper historical context allows us to be open to a different interpretation. It urges us to change our patriarchal lenses and reverse our thinking. We can find this story is life changing with an open heart and a new view.

It's far more than a story of a bad woman turned good. It is not just a story of missions and evangelism, but a story of God's love for the outcasts and downtrodden. It tells of a love so great that Jesus breaks the customs and traditions of the day to rescue and give new life to one soul judged as unlovely, unlovable and undeserving.

Ever since I can remember, the Woman at the Well has gotten a bad rap. She's been criticized for having five husbands and thought to be a harlot, but perhaps her story is simply a metaphor that represents more than gender. I'm suggesting that her story represents what it is to be "othered" and marginalized in society. It is a lesson about reaching out to those who are not like us.

I can image her telling her story:

Please don't act as if you don't know me. Everyone does. Even without a name, I am known. They never call my name, only the Samaritan Woman or the Woman at the Well. Of course, that tells you two things, right? First that I'm not important and second, that I could be anybody. I could even be you! Nina of NJ or Tina of Tennessee, Wendy by the well. Whoever. I think you get the picture. I could be you–ignored and unimportant.

They say I'm a whore because I've had five husbands. Ridiculous! Yes, I've had five husbands, but if the truth be told, I didn't choose–no, not one of them. Women rarely choose. My father arranged my first marriage for a small dowry. My happiness was never, ever a consideration.

The Pearl of God's Eye

My first husband died not long after we were married and as the law demanded, I was passed onto his brother. The custom was called Levirate marriage and it was supposed to protect widows and our children because most of us couldn't even earn a wage for our labor. Anyway, he soon grew weary of the added responsibility and passed me on to another brother. I went from one to the other, one to the other, but what can I say? A woman has got to eat and feed her children, right?

The one I'm with now is not my husband. I'll admit, I trade a lot of work and a little sex for a roof over my head and some food on my table. He won't marry me, but he pays the bills.

That's why I was at the well at noon. Work! I did my early morning haul, and I'll do the evening haul, too. I wasn't trying to avoid anyone. Trust me this village is far too small for that. I was just doing my day's work. Can I confess something? I feel trapped–really trapped.

So anyway, a couple of days ago, I took the long trek to haul water for the second time that day. As I approached the well, there was a man sitting on the well. I recognize his clothing. He was a Jew, a rabbi, and he asked me for water. What? You know that Jews have nothing to do with Samaritans and rabbis don't speak to women in public spaces. It was just the way things were.

I was stupefied! But what really blew my mind was that he has nothing to draw with. So, I'm thinking, "Dude, if you drink from my cup, you're going to be defiled. Ritually unclean for days!" But I was also intrigued, and I reminded him that he had nothing to drink from. Then he said that if you knew the gift of God, you would ask me for "living water." I thought, you have nothing to draw with! How could you possibly give me living water? And this gift of God? What was this?

I hadn't had the greatest education, and they didn't allow me to hang out in the Temple very often, but I was smart. Really, I was. I listened very well. So, with my quick, sarcastic wit, I challenged his theology, thinking, I bet he doesn't know much about our father, Jacob. But he kept challenging me with this living water and never thirsting again. In a few easy seconds, I was thinking about how I could get this living water and never come back here again. I would never, ever need to work this hard again!

Just as I asked, he wanted to get all in my business and asked about my husbands. But I could sense his kindness and compassion, and I was compelled to tell the truth, the whole truth. I began to sense that he was a prophet. I mean, how else could he possibly know these things? So, I put him to the test. I challenged him about where worship is to take place, and he told me that I don't even know what I worship! The nerve of Him! Really?

He said that God is looking for people who will worship him in Spirit and truth. I retorted that I knew about the Messiah and the Messiah was going to straighten all this mess out. Umphhh! He said that he was the Messiah. I knew it! I knew it! He *is* a prophet! I believed him. I knew it!

Jews don't come through Samaria and Rabbis don't speak to women in public, but he was just so kind and compassionate. I had to tell everybody because somehow, something in me had changed. Indeed, He is Christ.

You know, this wasn't just about finding me, a woman. No! It was much bigger than that. Think about it. I am a woman, a half-bred Jew, who lives in Samaria with a man who is not my husband. Despite all that, Jesus not only came my way, but came my way on purpose. He *needed* water from my cup, too. Drinking from my cup was an intimate act. With that gesture, I knew he was inviting me into his heart.

Look! God broke through. According to the society, I was the wrong gender, lived in the wrong zip code, was in the wrong relationship and was in the wrong religion–but, GOD BROKE THROUGH. God transcended society's norms and found me!

Have you ever felt like an isolated misfit, or marginalized and minimized because of your race, gender, the city where you live or because you're in an unconventional relationship? Are you just going through the motions of living and hoping to find the place where you fit? I've got good news for you! Just as Jesus found the Woman at the Well, no matter who you are or where you live, Jesus can find you, too.

11
Tamar

Nowhere is Safe
Background text: Exodus 22:16 and
Deuteronomy 22:28-29, 2 Samuel 13:1-22

What happens when familial boundaries are crossed? Tamar's story comes with a TRIGGER WARNING. Her story has been shrouded in silence and shame for the women and men who share it. While so many perpetrators and victims of sexual assault and incest seem to live their lives "business as usual," Tamar's story reminds us that God is omniscient and omnipresent. What many have tried to forget is never forgotten by God.

Tamar, Amnon and Absalom were the children of King David. Tamar was as beautiful as her brother Absalom was handsome. Like many women, her beauty and her curvaceous body was her burden. Her half-brother Amnon became so obsessed with her beauty that he made himself sick with imagination. He wanted her. He was a male, a prince and felt entitled.

Amnon's desire for Tamar was so intense that it began to consume him. Amnon appeared distracted more and more each day. His cousin Jonadab became quite curious about what was making him so irritable. Amnon confessed that he was in love with his sister, Tamar.

Jonadab was not disturbed by Amnon's desire. He took no thought for Tamar but conspired against her. He devised a cunning scheme to help Amnon. He told Amnon to feign sickness so that the king would send Tamar to prepare him a meal. Once she arrived, Amnon would have the opportunity to carry out the plan to rape her.

King David agreed to send Tamar to prepare cakes for her brother. Amnon not only wanted her to cook, but he also wanted to see her cook and eat from her hand. He repeated his desire for her to be "in my sight" three times.

Everything about Amnon's request alludes to his voyeur instinct and his desire to satisfy the male gaze. Everything about this text reeks of lust and lechery. The Orthodox Jewish Bible translates the cakes as heart-shaped, which further alludes to erotic passion.

Tamar complied with her father's wishes. She may be royalty, but she was still subject to her father and king. She busied herself in the kitchen and prepared the perfect cakes. Amnon insisted that she bring them into his bedroom and feed him from her hand.

He lured her in, took hold of her and begged her to lay with him. She was trapped. Tamar pleaded with Amnon to not force himself upon her because nothing like this should happen in Israel. It was disgraceful! "You will be like a fool," she insists. "Why don't you just ask the king if you can marry me?" Amnon does not heed her agitated cries.

He violated her despite her pleas. When all that he imagined was completed, he despised her and disposed of her. He called his servants and removed her from his home. She was left shrouded with shame, isolated and disgraced like many victims of sexual assault.

Tamar was shocked, shattered, shamed and silenced. Like so many, she was dismissed and left in desolation and despair. She quietly dressed herself in ashes and tore her garments. She was broken. Her brother, Absalom, suspected what had happened and counseled her to hold her peace. He advised that Amnon was her brother and she should not take the matter to heart. But seeing Tamar's woundedness, Absalom hated Amnon and despised him for what he had done to Tamar.

According to the law, Amnon should have been required to marry her, but like so many persons of privilege, he skirted the law. Instead of the honor of marriage, he objectified her, commodified her and threw her away. He never recognized her humanity.

Although marriage may seem to have been further punishment for the innocent Tamar, it was really a form of protection because the chances of a woman who was not a virgin being married were slim. Marriage guaranteed that she would have a means of support for the rest of her life.

Amnon abused his privilege as the king's son and King David abused his power as the king by not demanding justice or restitution on Tamar's behalf. Perhaps his indiscretion with Bathsheba had left him with some residual guilt and he could not confront Amnon. Or maybe he was reminded that there would never be peace in his house again. Power can be abused directly by the one who holds it or indirectly by those who are related to or associated with the powerful. In this care, it was both.

Like most family secrets, we don't grow up hearing the story of Tamar. Most brothers have affection for their sisters and work hard to protect them. Tamar's brother had much more than brotherly love; he had a passionate yearning and a lustful desire.

Sibling sexual assault is not well documented, but it is believed to be far more prevalent than adult-child sexual assault because it is usually dismissed as childhood curiosity. Research shows that there is lasting trauma and damaging effects for those involved in sibling incest. Often attention is given to adult-child sexual abuse, while victims of sibling abuse remain unseen and unheard, waiting for someone to uncover their injuries. The stigma causes victims to hide it from family members, neighbors and authorities so it most often goes unnoticed and unpunished.

God leaves us with this story to remind us that nothing escapes God's range of vision or understanding. What humanity may sweep under the rug is not forgotten by God. In Christ, we can find healing and restoration.

Two years after Tamar's experience, her brother Absalom took justice into his own hands and killed Amnon. We cannot justify his actions. Vengeance still belongs to God. However, we can be confident that Jesus, our elder brother, will mete out justice on our behalf, too.

12
Vashti

Holy Audacity and Royal Resistance:
Owning Your Body
Background text: Esther 1

Vashti is another woman left without a voice. In her role as the king's wife, she is valued for her beauty and her body. She is silent throughout the entire narrative. We don't even hear her refusal. Tired of being subjugated, exploited and overlooked, she took one bold step of resistance that changed the trajectory of her life. She could have allowed her husband's drunkenness to excuse his behavior again, but instead, she simply and silently refused his call.

By any standard, Vashti, had the life many women yearn for. She was King Ahasuerus' queen. Her refusal to appear before the king's court to show her beauty caused her to be banished from the palace. She lost her status as queen, her home, financial security and her friends. Where she went, we don't know. We never heard from her or about her again. Like so many women who stand up for themselves, life often changes drastically.

We often hear her portrayed as a wicked and disobedient woman, full of vanity and the sass that wrecks good marriages, negatively influences other women and enrages the hearts of men. I don't know what happened that day that made her believe she had enough. Could it be that she had an awakening to her own honor, dignity, and worth? Was she waiting to be respected and treated fully as a human being and waiting was no longer an option?

For some of us, Vashti is an icon of women's resistance. She operates from a place of personal power, tinged with a bit of righteous indignation, which makes the surrounding men angry that their power, position, and privilege had been challenged. How dare she?

The king's demands started long before the party. King Ahasuerus ruled over 127 provinces from India to Ethiopia. He decided to host the party of all parties by entertaining all his officials and his servants. This party lasted for six months! He celebrated with the nobles and the officials of the province and then spent a week celebrating with all the people of Shushan–the great and the small, the nobles and the peasants--on the front lawn of the palace.

While the king was entertaining the men on the front lawn, Queen Vashti entertained the women in the palace. The text speaks very specifically that the king owned the palace. This alludes to Vashti owning nothing, not even herself.

The royal wine was flowing endlessly. The king knew how to give a party! The guests were served in golden vessels, and no one was excluded. No one was compelled to drink, but those who chose to drink did so until their hearts content. Some were feeling no pain; they were stewed, stoned and intoxicated.

In a drunken haze, Ahasuerus demanded that his seven eunuchs bring Queen Vashti before him and the other men wearing her royal crown. Some suggest that Vashti was summoned to come to him wearing *only* her crown and others suggest she was to be dressed elegantly *with* her crown. The truth is it doesn't really matter. Whether fully dressed or naked and crowned, the reality is that she was summoned by the king to satisfy the male gaze–to experience the helpless humiliation of standing before a group of ogling men to satisfy the lust for power over the female frame granted to them by male privilege.

Vashti refused the king's order. She has had enough. She made a decision that cost her everything.

Everything. I am certain she knew the price of her "disobedience." The king was baffled, bewildered, offended and outraged. He decided to consult with his lawyers about the matter. What woman would dare disobey her husband, the king? What was to be done to her according to the law? The king's officials knew the implications of Vashti's refusal could resonate not only throughout the province but in their own homes. Something had to be done.

A royal order was sent out by the king and a law made that Vashti would never come before the king again and her position would be given to someone better than she. Better is best translated to mean better behaved. And it was made so, that all women would give honor (obey) their husbands, the small and the great. The King could have ended Vashti's life; after all, many had died for disobeying the king. Fortunately, she was only banished from the kingdom, which could be a small price to pay for one's own dignity.

Vashti's story is one most women can relate to. She appears to be valued more for her beauty than her brain. Despite her position, she was still objectified and commodified. No woman, no matter what she has achieved, is protected from this.

Street and workplace harassment are so common that we often just dismiss them as part and parcel of being a woman in the world. Being told to smile, enduring comments on our various body parts, hearing shouts of endearment from men as we walk in public are bad enough, but then we are denigrated if we ignore their calls or reject their attention.

Men "accidentally" touch women on trains, on the street, in stores as if women do not have a right to their own bodies. Women are expected to happily comply and remain pleasant and engaging, good humored and gracious at the very best and ignore and remain silent about the unwanted attention at the very least.

Vashti's story reminds us that some groups of men can be especially dangerous. Perhaps the king's response may have been different if he didn't have the influence of his seven high-ranking officials or if he was not embarrassed. Male violence and entitlement seem to escalate and gain momentum in groups.

Nevertheless, Vashti stood her ground. Women all around the world are standing up — for themselves and for their sisters. God is not mentioned anywhere in the book of Esther, but we know that God is there, just as God is with us. Sometimes we are like Vashti, and we boldly stand without regard to consequences. Sometimes we are not. We are reticent about speaking or standing up, but God is with us. We live, move and exist in God.

13
Woman with the Issue of Blood

Living on the Margins
Background text: Luke 8:40-48

This is a story not only of healing but of trusting God's ability in seemingly hopeless situations. What does it mean to risk everything for Jesus?

This nameless woman had an issue of blood. It was not just her monthly menstrual cycle, not at all. She had been bleeding steadily for twelve long years. Ritual purity was an impossibility. According to Jewish purity laws, she was unclean. She shouldn't have been out in the crowd. To touch her would mean to become ritually unclean.

Imagine, twelve years of longing for the embrace of your husband or wanting so desperately to hug your children. Talk about isolation! She could not even gather with her friends for a conversation while drawing water at the well. The loneliness was more than she could stand, not to mention the blood — the nagging trickling of blood. Listen, as she tells her own story.

I'm tired, weary and isolated. It's the blood. I'm talking about menstrual blood. It has been endless! What do you know about having a period for twelve years? Nothing! I bet you.

I am anemic, tired, grumpy and claustrophobic. Oh yeah, and lonely to boot! Some days it's just spotting and some days it just flows. Most of all, I hate the confinement. The hiding. I just must sneak out sometimes. It's been twelve endless years where days and nights pass by in a blur. I'm about to crawl up the walls in this little room — a room designed to separate me from everything and everyone I love.

The Gadarenes had come to trade. Through a tiny window, I overheard them talking about Jesus, miracles and the demon-possessed man who had been restored to his right mind. I was in awe, completely intrigued by the thought of meeting him. Could he help me? I was also feeling a little hopeless. It was about that law that made me unclean to everyone and everything.

I had sneaked out a few times, but these times were nothing like what I was imagining now. I really shouldn't take the chance of being seen by the Elders or Priests who typically followed Jesus. I don't know why because I heard that they don't even like him!

I thought, and I prayed; I prayed, and I thought. That was one advantage of being isolated —no interruptions. It took everything for me to gather the courage, but I decided to follow the crowd that day. I thought I had devised the perfect scheme to find my way into Jesus' presence without being noticed and causing much of a fuss.

The crowd that followed Jesus that day was a bit agitated and excited, so I crouched down and crawled into the crowd hoping to remain unseen. I didn't need to see his face or hear him speak. I thought if I could just touch his clothes, I'd be all right. They said he was a miracle worker, right? If he was who they said he was, then that would be enough. At that point, I felt that I didn't have a thing to lose! I had lost everything already.

Just as Jairus was pleading with Jesus to visit his sick daughter, I seized a perfect opportunity. I fell into the crowd just as he was passing, crouching, crawling, scratching and clawing the dirt. My eyes were scanning back and forth, back and forth. The crowd was enormous! The grit of the ground stuck to my sweaty hands, but I kept going.

Jesus was walking with focused determination, and mumbling something, maybe a prayer. He seemed distracted by the crowd. I pushed through, and I touched his robe. I knew instantly that I was healed. I thought this is great! I can now show myself to the priest and be done with this isolation.

Then, the unthinkable happened. Jesus quizzed the crowd, "Who touched me?" Filled with fear, I didn't answer. No one answered and then he bellowed, "Who touched me?" The disciples were so startled that one said sarcastically, "You see all these people! And you want to know who touched you?"

Jesus responded, "I felt power leave my body! Someone touched me!" At that point, I knew I couldn't hide any longer. I'd take whatever was to come. I was healed, and that was all that mattered. "It was me. I touched you." I began to tell him everything! With tender compassion, he looked at me and said, "Daughter, your faith has made you well. Go in peace." I didn't hesitate. I did just that, I went in peace — healed, whole and recovered.

Sadly, many women are still living on the margins of the society now. We don't hear much about it anymore, but HIV/AIDS is still impacting lives. While the number of women being diagnosed with HIV/AIDS has declined in recent years, African American women are disproportionately affected by HIV compared with women of other races. Of the total number of women living with HIV, approximately 60% are African American, 17% are white, and 17% are Latinx.[6]

Some factors that contribute to the HIV risk for women are not being aware that they are at risk, female physiology (women are simply more vulnerable because of their anatomy) and gender roles. It is important for women to be educated and aware of the risks and to know their status.

Like the Woman with the Issue of Blood, it's easy to be afraid and isolated. Thank God, Jesus knows no boundaries and calls no one "unclean." Whoever we are and whatever we may be afflicted with, we can press through the crowd and get to Him and find restoration and wholeness.

14
WOMEN OF JUDGES 19

VULNERABLE, VOICELESS VICTIMS OF VIOLENCE
BACKGROUND TEXT: JUDGES 19 AND 20

It doesn't matter where you live, oppression is global. Women are faced with domestic violence, human trafficking, clergy sexual misconduct, sexual assault, lower wages, street harassment — the list could go on and on. Is there anywhere that women are safe?

About 4,000 women die each year from violence inflicted by intimate partners, and another 1.3 million women are victims of sexual violence. Human trafficking affects about 20.9 million people who are forced into domestic service, the sex trade, other labor and child marriage. Beyond that, women from all religious group and denominations report that clergy sexual misconduct is on the increase. Where can women find safety?

The story of the women of Judges 19 may give rise to past trauma. It is known as a text of terror and tells the story of women who are vulnerable and powerless. Both are betrayed by every man they encounter — fathers, a husband and strangers. Surely it is a story that is difficult to hear, but it is a story many women live with or have lived through — violence at the hand of lovers and loved ones.

There were no judges in those days. Everyone was doing their own thing, whatever they thought was right. The prevailing attitude was, "It's all relative." The laws were ignored, there was no accountability, and violence and wickedness dominated the culture.

The main female character is a nameless woman who was the concubine (a secondary wife) to a Levite. The Levites served with the priests in the temple and were set apart as God's portion. They were dedicated to the sacred ritual duties in the tabernacle and throughout the land. The Levite is the only representative of God in this story.

Depending on who you want to believe and what translation you read, there is a version that says the concubine "played the whore" and left the Levite. In another version, she became "angry with him" and left. If she played the whore, we are left with a couple of questions that cast doubt on that interpretation.

First, if the woman were an adulterer, would her

father have welcomed her back into his home? This was a time when adultery was punishable by stoning and honor killing was a common practice. The text says that after some time, the Levite went to "speak kindly to her." Would he be kind if she had committed adultery or humiliated him? I don't think so. That seems highly unlikely because the male ego is fragile. Nevertheless, he went to speak to her, but the irony is that he never said a word to her. All his interaction and conversation were with her father. She was silent throughout the entire story.

The woman's father was happy to see the Levite and spent days entertaining him. Although we have no indication of her father's and the Levite's relationship, perhaps her father felt the additional burden of another person to provide for and no longer wanted her there. As for the woman, I imagine she may have been offended or even fearful and uncertain of how the Levite's visit would conclude.

After about five days, the Levite was intent on taking her back with him. Did she want to go? Who knows? We never heard her speak. Was this a transaction between her father and the Levite? Or was this human trafficking?

As it happened, the woman and the Levite were making their way back to Ephraim when night began to fall. They decided to seek lodging in Gibeah, the parcel of land that belonged to the tribe of Benjamin. The Bejamites were Israelites; they were God's people.

It was in Gibeah, among the Levite's own people, that the unthinkable happened. The Levite and the woman accepted the kindness of a gentleman who invited them into his home. This was not hanging out with strangers as we may think, but a common and expected practice among the Israelites.

As they began to settle in for the night with a little bread and a cup a tea, there came a jolting clamor from a crowd of men at the door. They wanted the Levite, and they did not want to talk. They wanted to have their way with him. They yelled to the old man, "Bring him out! Bring him out! We want him! Let us have him!" Appalled and disgusted, the old man and the Levite panicked. "Don't do this wicked thing. You can have my virgin daughter and this man's concubine and do whatever you want with them!" If justice dominated, raping women would be as wicked as raping men, but there was no justice. The Levite and man of Gibeah threw the women out that night, disposing of them like merchandise, mere chattel.

We never find out what happened to the virgin daughter. We can only imagine the worst. We do know that the concubine was gang-raped and tortured all night. Not one man saw her humanity or that she, too, was made in the image of God. She was just a commodity.

The woman made her way back to the house, clawing and groveling through the dirt streets, gravel sticking to her hands and forearms. She fell in and out of consciousness upon the threshold. Was she dead, or had she lost consciousness? We are never told.

The Levite found her in the morning. He took her limp body, hoisted it upon his donkey and began the tedious journey back to Ephraim. In a moment of regret, the Levite became enraged—the one emotion that men can feel and be safely viewed as men. It seemed the closer he got to home, the angrier he became. Perhaps he is angry with himself. The conflict of being the priest he was called to be and the wicked man that he had become was too great.

When the Levite reached Ephraim, his fierce, hot anger erupted. His boiling anger spilled onto her body as he began to carve her into twelve pieces—one for each tribe of Israel—and sent the pieces throughout the land. Perhaps the gruesome packages were sent to stir the tribes into God-consciousness again. It certainly provoked conversation because everyone who knew of the crime began to talk about it. "When he got home, he took a butcher knife and cut her body into twelve pieces. Then he told some messengers, 'Take one piece to each tribe of Israel and ask everyone if anything like this has ever happened since Israel left Egypt. Tell them to think about it, talk it over, and tell us what should be done?'" Everyone who saw a piece of the body said, "This is horrible! Nothing like this has ever happened since the day Israel left Egypt."[7]

All the tribes of Israel except for Benjamin united and decided to have the men who raped and murdered the woman put to death. However, when they confronted the people of Benjamin, they chose to protect the guilty men rather than allow justice to be served. Eventually, a civil war erupted, and the tribe of Benjamin was defeated. All but 600 men of Benjamin were killed.

Like so many women today, this woman did not receive justice—even in death. Far too often men who rape and batter are protected, and women victimized by them are slandered and disgraced. The incidences of intimate partner violence are so great that if it were classified as a disease, it would be considered a pandemic. The World Health Organization (WHO) reports that upwards of 75% of women report experiencing emotional abuse while 61% report experiencing some form of physical abuse globally. It is a public health issue.[8]

This terrifying story reminds us that God has not forgotten us, and God will vindicate us. However, we are most often the vessels that God will use for the victory. We must be willing to use our voices to confront injustice of any kind. We must also be willing to become our own saviors. Our words are the fountainhead of change. Use your voice. Speak up. Speak out. If we don't save us, no one will.

15
Zelophehad's Daughters

When Women Unite
Background text: Numbers 26:33, 51-56; 27:1-8, 36:1-9

Embedded within the history of Israel's strife with God, we find a God who calls for justice for all. When Zelophehad's daughters find themselves on the losing end of the inheritance law, they stood before God and their congregation to challenge such injustice. They challenged the law that would have left them with nothing from their father's land.

Zelophehad's daughters leave us with an impressive lesson that women can accomplish much when they stand together in unity. I can only imagine the courage it took to not only face their leader, Moses, but their entire congregation to ask for their inheritance. To know that God quickly responded in the affirmative asserts God's amazing love for women and girls.

Zelophehad laid on his deathbed, trembling with fever. He could not help but wonder what would become of his daughters, especially with no brothers to look out for their best interests. He blessed each of them by name -- Mahlah, Noah, Hoglah, Milcah, and Tirzah -- and prayed that they would find good husbands.

Soon after Zelophehad's death, the Lord commanded Moses and Eleazer, the priest, to take a census of the people of Israel, twenty years old and older, who had come out of Egypt. They were to be counted according to the lineage of their fathers.

Each tribe was given its inheritance based on its size. The larger the tribe, the larger their inheritance property would be. The inheritance laws had always demanded that the property rights come through men and be given to men – no ifs, ands, or buts about it.

Israel, like everywhere else in the known world, was steeped in patriarchy. Men dominated, violence prevailed, religion kept women in their places, and whoever won in war by snatching and exploiting the land and the people were declared the winners.

Moses began the census and distribution of land. The descendants of Rueben. Check. The descendants of Simeon. Check. The children of Gad. Check. On and on it went. Twenty-three thousand people in all, except those who were lost in the wilderness.

When all was said and done, the daughters of Zelophehad came forward. Their father was a member of the Manassite clan. They made it clear that their father had died in the wilderness but was not among those who had rebelled against the Lord and then they asked the question, "Should our father's name be lost among the clans and receive no inheritance because he had no son?" Moses went before the Lord, and the Lord said, "The daughters of Zelophehad are right in what they are saying; you shall indeed let them possess an inheritance among their father's brothers and pass the inheritance of their father on to them."

Can you imagine? Together, five women challenged God and men to justice and to circumvent the law. They were brazened and brassy with just the right amount of holy boldness to raise the question at all. But to raise the question openly in the church?! Let's just say they are my sheroes!

The most amazing part of the story is how God responded by saying, "Zelophehad's daughters speak what is right. Give them the land and make sure you tell the Israelites that this is how it should be." Well, not exactly like that but that was the sum and substance of God's response.

What a stunning victory! This story teaches us that we can influence God and lets us know that God will speak on our behalf. God acted in the sphere of what was not socially acceptable because God honored humanity's dominion over the land. God did not interfere until God was invited to play a part. We see that principal demonstrated when the Israelites were oppressed by Egyptians and a deliverer was sent only after they cried out to God.

Unfortunately, their victory comes with consequences. We later find out that the "chief fathers" gathered before Moses and other male leaders. Although they were quite clear about the commandment concerning the sisters and their inheritance property, they were afraid the women would take their property with them when they married. That would mean another tribe could gain property rights.

Unlike the women's request, the men's gathering did not take place in the temple or among the people. In fact, there was nothing religious or sacred about it. It was a business meeting. We don't observe Moses talking to the Lord about it, but we do note Moses speaking on behalf of the Lord.

Did he use "prophetic license" to speak on behalf of God as we often see Paul doing in the New Testament? What Moses speaks from the Lord poses an arresting limit to the women's freedom. They are free to marry whoever they think best—if the men are from their father's tribe. Essentially, they can inherit the property, but can only keep it by marrying a cousin. If they decided to marry out of the clan, they would lose the rights to their property. The sisters consented and agreed to marry within the tribe. This was not the perfect triumph, but a victory, nevertheless.

Like many instances in life, women are most often asked to compromise and make trade-offs that men do not have to make. We still live in a world where it seems we take one step forward and two steps backward in challenging the status quo. I can only imagine the bravery and determination it took those sisters to stand. Through this story, God not only demonstrated God's justice but God's awesome love for women.

Some Final Thoughts

I don't know about you, but I am completely astounded when I realize just how much God loves me. So many times, in the rhythm of an ordinary day, someone somewhere seems to remind me that in the grand scheme of things, I am *just* a woman.

Whether I'm getting the car repaired, at the grocery store, teaching in a classroom or walking down the street, there is an easy insinuation that I'm a little less than. Small and unimportant — the consequence of being born in a female body. Well, God always reminds me that I am truly beloved. In fact, I am the pearl of God's eye.

Didn't Jesus find it necessary to get to Samaria with a determined stride just to meet a woman? And what about the woman caught in adultery? (I'm still trying to find the man.) Didn't he disperse the crowd with a simple question and meet her with compassion? How about Mary Magdalene? She has always gotten a bad rap but was the first to see Jesus after the resurrection.

I think that's enough to let you know that woman was not an afterthought, created to bring satisfaction to a man. No, not at all. You matter! You were created to be comparable (similar, worthy of comparison) companions, to walk side-by-side with man.

"So, God created human beings [man; the Hebrew Adam can mean human beings, humankind, person, man, or the proper name Adam] in his image [reflecting God's nature/character and representing him in the world]. In the image of God, he created them. He created them male and female."[9] (*Expanded Bible*, Genesis 1:27)

God said it wasn't good for Adam to be alone, probably because God knew that he would get lost in the garden and not ask for directions! But really, it was not good for man to be alone because together man and woman could experience a better oneness.

It was not that Adam was not complete without Eve or Eve without Adam. Both were made in the image and likeness of God and complete in themselves. However, men and women have inherent characteristics that can make a very complementary relationship. Walking shoulder to shoulder, they form a union so commanding and compelling that it unfolds the splendor of God's loving relationship with the church. Together, they were a better one.

So, my dear sisters, Daughters of Zion, God is

calling you for great and greater things. You're not stuck in "your place." You don't do what you do "well for a girl" and you don't have to "smile" unless you are wonderfully delighted.

Listen, sister, you're not the problem. No way! You are gifted, talented and you create solutions to problems. You're not just another pretty face. God fashioned you to be brassy, brainy *and* beautiful!

"He took the twelve-year-old girl by the hand and said, "Talitha, koum!" which means, "Little girl, get up!"[10] (Mark 5:41)

So, I say to you, get up, sister, get up! The fullness of life awaits you. Jesus wants to take your hand and escort you into your dreams. God still exceeds with abundance all we can ask or imagine. It is time to get up, sister, get up!

If you would like to connect with women who are re-visioning their lives, you can find us on Facebook at www.facebook.com/groups/revisionwomen/. Learn more about ReVision Ministries at www.revision-ministries.org and www.revisionwomen.com. I'd welcome the opportunity to connect with you!

Peace and blessings,

Simone

About the Author

Simone Oliver has ReVisioned her life from tragedy to triumph, from victim to victor and from broken to beautiful through God's grace and unfailing love. She is an ordained minister and passionate preacher, educator, life coach and advocate for women whose pragmatic, earthy style reaches the heart of an issue. Simone is committed to the spiritual care of women and girls, bringing healing to wounded hearts by God's grace and finding solutions to gender-based violence through prevention and awareness education. Simone is a powerful preacher of the Gospel and a gifted empowerment speaker and facilitator.

Simone's avid interest in reading and the power of language led her to complete her undergraduate education at New Jersey City University earning a BA in English/Literature. She taught English and Reading in the public school system and was a featured educator on New Jersey Classroom Close-up. She received her Master of Divinity degree from Princeton Theological

Seminary with a certificate in Women's Studies and was the recipient of the John Allen Swink Award for Excellence in Preaching.

Simone, along with her husband Allen, founded ReVision Ministries (formerly New Day Ministries) in 2012. They work to empower women and girls to reach their highest potential while educating houses of worship on ways to fully embrace feminine gifts and become safe spaces free of harassment and abuse. ReVision Ministries offers a variety of workshops to women and religious leaders, including Domestic Violence Awareness and a SAFE Worship Spaces program. In addition, she hosts ReVision Women, an online women's support group and facilitates local and online Bible studies.

Simone is the author of *From Grace to Grace: A Prayer & Healing Journal*; and has written for the blogs *For Harriet* and *Blessed Chix*. She has co-authored three anthologies, *Gumbo for the Soul: The Recipe for Literacy in the Black Community*, *In Realitea, She is Me* and *God Said I Am Battle Scar Free,* an Amazon Best Seller. She was an honored recipient of the Phoenix Award from Harambe Social Services for her work in the field of domestic violence. Simone is a member of the Women of Color Network, NJ State Coalition to End Domestic Violence and the National Council of Negro Women; however, her greatest joy is life with her husband and daughter.

Works Cited

1. The Holy Bible: Contemporary English Version. American Bible Society, 1995.

2. The Holy Bible: Contemporary English Version. American Bible Society, 1995.

3. MacNeil, Natalie. "Entrepreneurship Is the New Women's Movement." Forbes, Forbes Magazine, 25 Sept. 2014, https://www.forbes.com/sites/work-in-progress/2012/06/08/entrepreneurship-is-the-new-womens-movement/#5efbf1b03b4c.

4. DuMonthier, Asha, et al. The Status of Black Women in the United States. The Status of Black Women in the United States, https://iwpr.org/publications/status-black-women-united-states-report/.

5. Kasinof, Laura. "Women, War and PTSD." Washington Monthly, https://washingtonmonthly.com/magazine/novdec-2013/women-war-and-ptsd/

6. Shropshre, Terry, et al. "Why HIV and AIDS Affect Black Women Disproportionately." Rolling Out, 2 Apr. 2012, https://rollingout.com/2012/04/02/why-hiv-and-aids-affect-black-women-disproportionately/.

7. The Holy Bible: Contemporary English Version. American Bible Society, 1995.

8. "Violence Against Women." World Health Organization, Global Health Observatory (GHO) Data, https://www.who.int/gho/women_and_health/violence/en/.

9. Expanded Bible, Thomas Nelson, 2011.

10. The Holy Bible: Contemporary English Version. American Bible Society, 1995.

www.ingramcontent.com/pod-product-compliance
Lightning Source LLC
Chambersburg PA
CBHW031818110426
42743CB00057B/853